What a joyful, imaginative, and heartwarming adventure this book is! The Little Inventor is a beautiful celebration of creativity, family, and the incredible power of a child's imagination. As I turned each page, I could feel the deep love that inspired this story—it shines through every word, every invention, and every memory shared between Chase, Cameron, and their beloved Pappy.

Valene Stone has captured something truly magical here. I love how this story encourages young minds to build, explore, and believe in their ideas. It's a tribute not only to her brilliant sons but to every child who dares to dream and every parent who cheers them on.

I especially loved the ending—and I won't give it away—but it left me smiling with my heart full. This book belongs on every family's bookshelf.

—Dr. Peggy McColl, *New York Times Bestselling Author*

A delightful, empowering read that shows kids their ideas can become reality. As a fellow children's author, I love how this story inspires creativity and confidence—for kids and parents alike.

— **Vicky McGrath,** *Bestselling Author of*
The Dragon and the Mysterious Artifact

Valene's The Little Inventor is a joyful celebration of curiosity, creativity, and the fearless imagination of childhood. Through Chase's inventive escapades, young readers are encouraged to embrace the wonder of making, building, and dreaming—no matter how messy or unconventional the process may be. This charming story not only inspires children to see possibilities everywhere but also reminds parents of the incredible things that can happen when we simply give children the space to explore. A vibrant and uplifting read that champions every child's inner inventor. Your child will love it!

— **Vladimira Kuna, Elite Mind Alchemist,**
Award Winning & 3 x International Bestselling author
of Thunderbird's Mystical Feather, In the Realm of the Magic Ruby
and The Bible of the Masterminds, Faith Building Podcast Host

'The Little Inventor' is a heartwarming story of a little boy name Chase who is not afraid to use his imagination and talent to create inventions. With help and encouragement from his 'Mom' and 'Pappy' , he builds not one, not two, but many inventions that will help make life easier for someone he knows. This book is a must in everyone's home who want to see their children use their talents to become the person they were meant to be.

— **Louise Malecha,** *International Best Author of 'Going to Papa and Nana's Farm' and 'Ginger's Big Day'*

Chase's inventive adventures beautifully show how creativity and problem-solving can turn simple ideas into impactful creations. This book is an inspiring reminder that with a little imagination and a lot of heart, the possibilities are endless. A must-read for parents and kids alike!

— **Judy O'Beirn,** *President and CEO of Hasmark Publishing*

The Little
INVENTOR

Written by:
VALENE STONE

Published by:
Hasmark Publishing International
www.hasmarkpublishing.com

Editor:

Cover Design: Anne Karklins (anne@hasmarkpublishing.com)

Interior Layout: Amit Dey (amit@hasmarkpublishing.com)

ISBN 13: 978-1-77482-291-3
ISBN 10: 1-77482-291-1

Dedication

Dedicated to my beautiful sons, Chase and Cameron. Your love, joy, creativity, and imagination have inspired me to be the best Mom and person I can be.

In loving memory of Dad, Chase, and Cameron's Pappy, who loved building and creating with the boys and me.

Special dedication to my grandfather, Herbert T. Stone Jr., who was a train engineer and shared his love & passion for trains with all his grandchildren.

At the young age of two,
with his big eyes so blue,

this little boy started being
a little inventor.

The little inventor named Chase began to create

with cardboard, cans, boxes, popsicle sticks, tape, & lace

With anything, he could create a great invention!

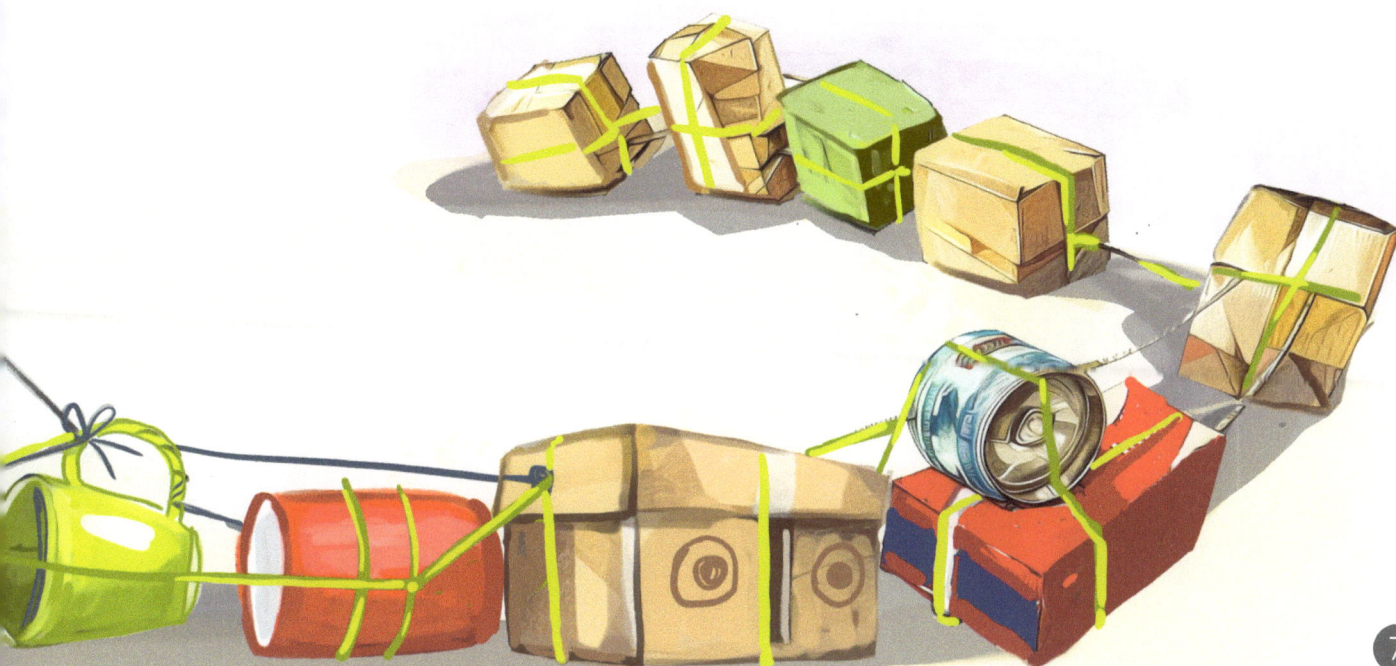

Yes! There would be a mess all over the place....

To witness the smile on this young child's face was enough for Mama to leave everything in its place.

From the young age of three,
Chase's fascination with trains grew, and
he smiled with glee as he put together his first train tracks.

Like his Great-Granddady before him, he built
so many train track configurations around the house....
especially on and around the dining room table.

CAUTION! TRAIN TRACKS EVERYWHERE!

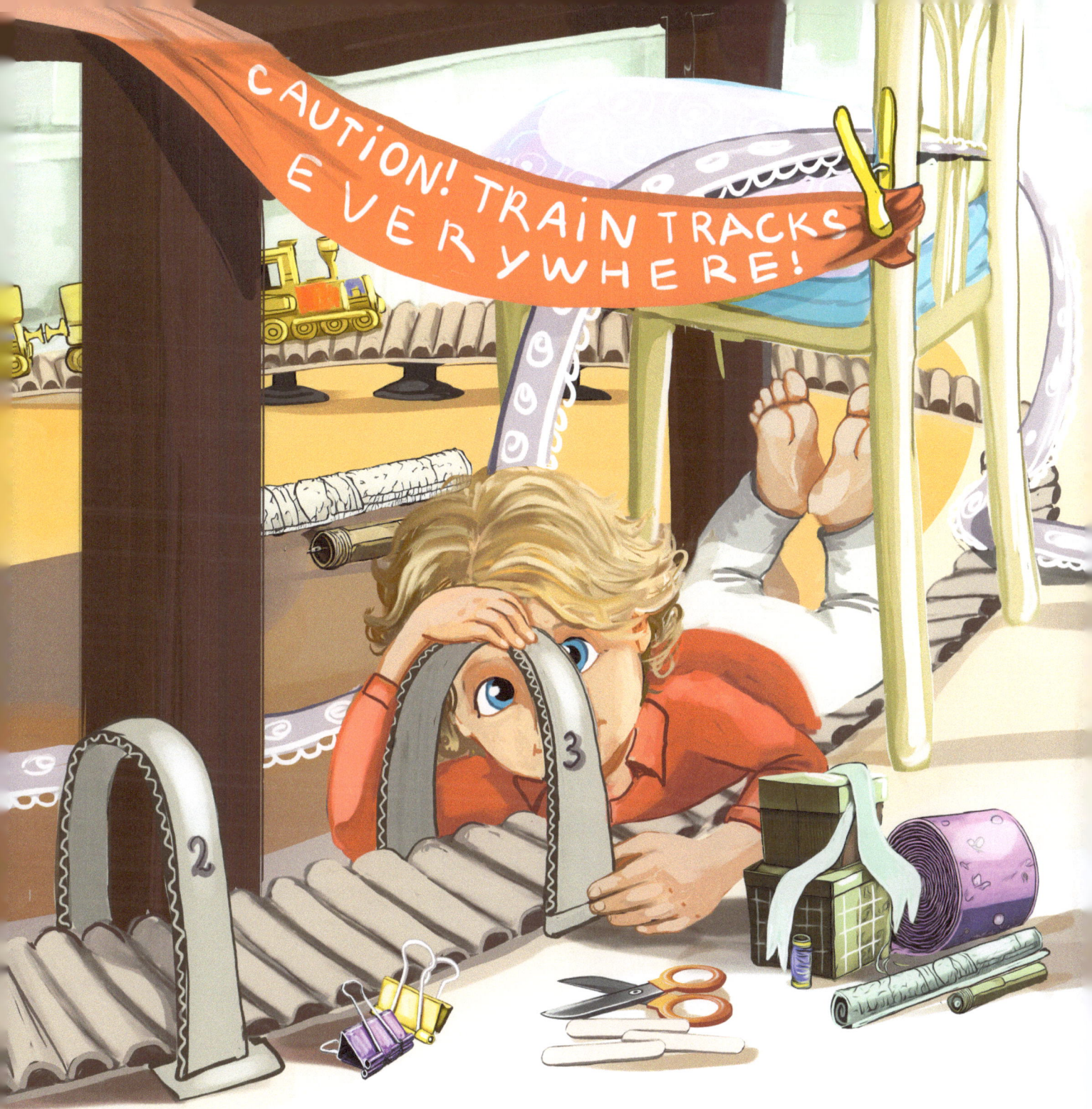

It was not always easy to put together train tracks and make the trains run smoothly on the tracks...this was frustrating. Chase's little brother, Cameron, was always right by his side, building and playing with the trains, and he would help secure the tracks.

One day, just in time for dinner, Cameron looked out the window, at the beautiful snow-covered trees and announced, "Pappy's here!" Chase and Cameron ran to Pappy and gave him a big hug. "Hi, Chase and Cameron!" said Pappy.

"Hi, Pappy! We need you! We are having some trouble. Please help us get these train tracks built smoothly."

Pappy jumped right in and helped secure the tracks.
For every train configuration Chase created and built,
he made cardboard tunnels and bridges—not just
one, but sometimes two, three or even four! He was
so excited to show his bridges and tunnels to Pappy!
Of course, Pappy loved them, and together, they built
even more tracks, bridges and tunnels.

Cameron was so excited to experience this dinner-time fun with Chase. He loved helping his big brother create the most amazing train configurations!

One snowy day, while building a train station at dinner time, Mama set the table and served dinner all around the train-track-covered table. Chase and Cameron spotted cardinals and blue jays flying on and around their favorite tree outside the window.

One can imagine just how much eating was actually being done. Even Pappy looked at the table and said, "Boys, how are we supposed to eat around all of these tracks?" Pappy and Mama looked at Chase's proud smile. They both laughed and agreed to eat around the tracks.

When Chase was four, Mama and Dad signed Chase up for tee-ball.

When Chase arrived at the baseball field, he was not thrilled to play in the game and instead ran off the field.

Next, Chase tried soccer. Chase loved playing ball with family and friends — running, kicking, and throwing a ball around. Yet he was not thrilled about playing soccer games at that age.

This caused Mama to become curious and ask, "What would Chase love to do?"

When Chase was five, his love of building & creating grew. Mama signed Chase up for a kids' building group with architects!

When Chase and Cameron arrived at the builders' group, their eyes lit up.

Chase was so excited to build and create. He, of course, asked Cameron to join in on the fun, and the first assignment...

"The Skyscraper Challenge!!"

Chase and Cameron raced off to start collecting materials, much to Chase's delight.

"WOW!" Chase said. "Cam, look at all of these cool things to choose from!"

As Chase and Cameron gathered supplies, Chase said, "Look, that is the girl that lives next door, Keira!" Keira noticed them right away and ran over to their table. She said, "Hi, Chase and Cameron! May I team up and help build your skyscraper with you?!"

Chase replied, "Yes, of course you can help build, too."

Chase, Cameron, and Keira teamed up
and got to work building...

The most epic skyscraper ever!!

Chase was such a natural at this building challenge! As they were holding up the cardboard, Chase instructed Cameron to hold up the walls as he glued. It was a challenge for Chase and Cameron to figure out how to use the hot glue gun carefully and not burn their hands. Keira had experience and demonstrated how to glue safely. She cheered Chase and Cameron on as they completed the project together as a team!

It was Chase and Cameron's first time using a
hot glue gun to create — and, wow, they had fun!
When the building time was over, Chase, Cameron, Keira,
and the other kids stood up to present their creations.

Chase presented their skyscraper, and he did great!
It was on this day that Mama and Dad realized Chase
had found a true gift and passion!

Chase's love for building, creating, and inventing flourished.

One sunny day at home, at the age of six, Chase asked, "Mama, do you need a place to store charger plugs and chords?" "Yes, sure, Chase!" said Mama. And Chase and Cameron took off creating and building a... Charger Station Caddy.

Keira stopped over to play and asked, "Wow, what are you two creating?" She jumped right in to help paint and decorate the custom-made charger station caddy with pretty colors and labeled it "Mom".

If there is a problem, leave it to Chase to create something great!

On a lovely spring day, Chase walked into the kitchen and noticed the pretty pink flower petals starting to bloom on his favorite tree outside the window. He grabbed an apple out of the wire basket on the wall and called out, "Mama! There are a bunch of fruit flies flying around all of the fruit! I am going to build a fruit-fly trap and help capture these flies. Is that ok, Mama?" "Yes, Chase! That would be so helpful."

Chase called out to Cameron, and they set off to the creation station to begin building! Cameron had a plan for a container to start with, and Chase was amazed and impressed by his little brother being so creative and helpful!

Together they built the most efficient fruit-fly trap! They had fun monitoring the number of flies that were trapped.

Mama was so grateful for her little boys, and for their creativity and thoughtfulness in helping to solve problems around the house.

One sunny fall day, while changing batteries on a train at the age of seven,

Chase said, "Mama, do you need a place to store used batteries — so we can bring them to a recycled battery store?"

"Yes, sweetie! That would be great!"

Chase and Cameron went next door to find Keira.

Together at the creation station in the mudroom, Chase, Cameron, and Keira got ready to build and create a special box labeled:

BATTERY-EATER 2000

That was not all...Chase, Cameron, and Keira built another, and another, and another Battery-Eater 2000s!!

"Mama, look! We made a bunch of my Battery-Eater 2000s!" Chase shouted with glee. "Mama, people need these!"

Chase said to Cameron and Keira, "Let's make a sign, get a table, and sell these out on the lawn!!"

"Wow, sweetie!" said Mama. "That is super creative, inventive, and helpful to others. Go for it!"

And off they went...

Chase was busy creating a plan, and with the help of Cameron and Keira, he began putting it into action.

They set up a spot on the lawn to sell the Battery-Eater 2000s. The pumpkins and Halloween decorations along the driveway added a nice touch.

Chase and Cameron were so excited to see that
the first customer to pull up to the selling table
was Pappy! Pappy got out of his truck and hugged
Chase and Cameron. Chase and Cameron greeted
Pappy and introduced him to Keira. Chase told him
all about the special boxes and how they worked.

"Wow, Chase! What a cool idea! How much are you charging for your Battery-Eater 2000s? I need one. I have lots of used batteries at home."

Chase replied, "They are $7 each."
The kids were thrilled to make their first sale!
They realized creating and selling was so much fun.

Little Chase was always determined to create and invent something great to solve a problem and help others. While Pappy visited, they sat down for dinner with the train-track table stations. Chase had an idea to invent a solar-powered soda-can car. He began creating his invention plan.

Chase asked Cameron to help gather supplies to get ready to create.

Led by Chase, Pappy and Cameron worked together to build a really fast and cool solar-powered soda-can car! As they got started, Chase needed some help attaching the wires properly, so Pappy helped guide him. Pappy assisted Cameron in attaching the wheels, and then Cameron worked on aligning them. Together they built a super fast, solar-powered, soda-can car based on Chase's vision!

They played with the car together in the backyard.
Chase and Cameron loved when Pappy visited,
as he always helped them build and create.

Early one summer morning when Chase was eight, they were playing soccer in the backyard.

While hanging out with the turkeys that often visited their yard, Cameron created a drawing of a fidget device game and asked Chase if he could create it.

All based on his brother's vision and need...

This brilliant kid was on a mission to build and create a great invention all based on his brother's vision and need! Chase and Cameron were having so much fun creating and inventing, when Keira knocked on the back door.

"Hi, Chase and Cam!" she said. They greeted Keira and told her all about the invention they were working on. Keira asked, "May I join you in building this new invention?" "Yes," said Chase. "We would love for you to build with us!" Keira was happy to create and build with Chase and Cameron! So the three got busy creating, building, and inventing.

Mama watched in amazement as Chase created the plan for the invention. He, Cameron and Keira, took off to their creation station and began to create and build the prototype of the game device...

After quite some time building, Mama said, "Let's take a break and go to the beach, and get outdoors and move our bodies!"

It was a hot summer day, so mama took the three kids to the beach. They went swimming, played in the sand, and even had fun doing a dance workout together!

When they got home from the beach, Pappy stopped over for dinner. Pappy wanted to help build and create the fidget device game, so he ran to the store to gather some supplies for the new invention.

Together, they created a wonderful new invention!

At breakfast one morning when Chase was nine, Mama cooked French toast. She poured way too much maple syrup on Cameron's French toast because the spout on the bottle was too big.

"I've got an idea!" said Chase.

And off he went... to his creation station to build a... Maple Syrup Dispenser! It could also be used for small pets as a water dispenser!

Mama said, "Wow! This is so fantastic and helpful!

Thank you, Chase!"

On a rainy summer day, at the age of ten, Chase had an idea to create a soda-can food warmer.

Chase called to Cameron to help, and they went next door to get Keira. They set off to the creation station to gather supplies.

Chase presented the invention plan to the team, and together, with help from Cameron and Keira, they created and invented an awesome soda-can food warmer!

With Mama supervising, Chase warmed up mini s'mores and other yummy snacks for Keira and Cameron.

Chase was always creating and inventing something fantastic!

One day when Chase, Cameron, Keira, and Mama were outside jumping on the trampoline, Mama's tripod stand for her phone broke. She used it all the time.

Chase asked, "Mama, would you like me to create a new phone stand for you?"

"Yes, please. I would love that, Chase! I need one to film my outside workout in an hour."

Chase replied, "Ok, Mama. I am going to create a stand for you!"

Chase asked Cameron and Keira to help, and together they went to the creation station in the mudroom, where they gathered supplies to began creating and building.

There was a lot of cutting and use of the hot glue gun. Chase created a new custom-built phone tripod stand for his Mama.

But that's not all...

Chase and his team, Cameron and Keira, also created a detachable phone holder to prop up and use anywhere! Wow! Mama was amazed and grateful for her generous and inventive son and his team!

Chase went on to create a series of smartphone accessories.

When Chase received his first cellphone, he went straight to the creation station, building a phone case with a built-in stand.

He asked Cameron to help him glue and hold the parts together — and together they completed the case in less than ten minutes!

"Wow!" said Mama. "That is awesome, Chase and Cam. Now your phone will be safe, Chase!"

Mama hugged Chase and Cameron in amazement!

Keira arrived at the back door at Chase's creation station and said to Chase, "I love coming over here! You and Cameron are always creating and inventing something awesome!"

Chase replied, "You have been so great at building and creating with us! Girls are incredible inventors, too!"

Chase had so many ideas in his creative mind!

You, too, can create Something great... at any age!

WHEN AN IDEA POPS INTO YOUR MARVELOUS MIND, TAKE ACTION, AND YOU WILL AMAZE YOURSELF WITH WHAT YOU ARE CAPABLE OF CREATING!

FOR WITHIN YOUR BEAUTIFUL MIND IS YOUR INVISIBLE SUPERPOWER~

YOUR IMAGINATION!

Acknowledgements

I would love to express my heartfelt gratitude to
Peggy Mccoll, fellow author and mentor.
Your guidance, expertise and belief in me has helped
inspire me to take the leap of faith and step out as an
author! I am truly blessed to have you as my mentor!

I am truly grateful for Judy and the team at
Hasmark Publishing! Your expertise, and guidance
and encouragement in the journey of being
a children's book author has been incredible.

To my sons, Chase and Cameron: my biggest
accomplishment in this world is being your Mother,
and you both inspire me everyday! I would not be an
author without your creativity, inspiration, imagination,
love and support. I am forever grateful for you both,
and I look forward to watching you grow.